Baby Jesus is Born

Luke 2:1–20 for Children
Written by Gloria A. Truitt
Illustrated by Kathy Mitter

ARCH® Books
Copyright © 1994 Concordia Publishing House
3558 S. Jefferson Avenue, St. Louis, MO 63118-3968
Manufactured in the United States of America

There was a Roman emperor
    Two thousand years ago,
Who asked the folks he ruled to make
    A trip quite hard and slow.

All people had to travel to
    The town from where they came.
(So they could all be counted, each
    Was asked to sign his name.)

Now in the town of Nazareth—
In the land of Galilee—
There lived a man named Joseph and
His promised wife-to-be.

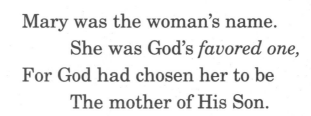

Mary was the woman's name.
　　She was God's *favored one*,
For God had chosen her to be
　　The mother of His Son.

Joseph knew he had to heed
The emperor's decree,
So he and Mary set out from
The land of Galilee.

At last they came to Bethlehem,
    A town of little size.
Now the streets were crowded, which
    Was not a great surprise!

Quickly Joseph found an inn,
    The only one in town,
For Mary was exhausted and
    She needed to lie down.

Joseph asked the innkeeper,
    "Do you have room for two?"
"No," he said to Joseph, who
    Then sighed, "What should I do?"

"I'm sorry," said the innkeeper,
   "I really am unable
To provide a room for you . . .
   But wait! I have a stable!"

Joseph looked at Mary, then
   He sadly shook his head.
"At least you will be safe from harm,
   And you can rest," he said.

Now, on that night our Lord was born
To save all folk on earth,
And that is why we still today
Observe His holy birth!

This baby was the promised King—
God's Son, this couple knew—
And so they named Him Jesus,
As God had told them to.

Some shepherds in a field nearby
Were tending to their flock,
When suddenly an angel came!
Imagine their great shock!

God's holy light surrounded them,
And they were so dismayed!
But then the angel of the Lord
Said, "Do not be afraid!

"I bring you good and joyous news
For everyone this day!
A Savior has been born to you!
To Him, go find your way.

"You'll find this baby wrapped in cloths
And lying in a manger.
You'll know Him by these signs and, so,
This Child won't be a stranger."

Then suddenly great numbers of
God's angels from the sky
Appeared and sang His praises,
"Glory be to God on high!"

The shepherds said to one another,
"Could this really be?
Our Savior born in Bethlehem?
Quick! Let's go and see!"

They hurried off and found the Child,
Just as the angel said,
Inside a humble stable with
A manger for His bed.

They knelt beside this holy Child,
    Then ran to spread the word,
Telling everyone they met
    Of what they'd seen and heard!

Dear Parents:

Take a minute with your child during the busy Christmas season to worship the Christ Child, born to be your Savior. After reading this story, act it out, using the figures from your crèche set. Assure your child of Jesus' great love—so great that He willingly exchanged His heavenly throne for a bed of straw and a cross.

Read the last page to your child again, explaining that the shepherds did not keep the good news of Jesus' birth to themselves. Invite friends or neighbors to your home for a Christmas devotion. Share with everyone around you the message that Jesus was born to be our Savior.

The Editor